Celebrating
Ayyám-i-Há
Around the World

Written and Illustrated by
Melissa López Charepoo

Dedicated with love to

Maxwell and Paul

This book intends to be an artistic representation

of the beauty and diversity of the human race,

rather than a specific and complete representation of the people,

traditional dresses, and languages you may find in different parts of the world.

Text and Illustrations

© 2017 Melissa López Charepoo

First published 2017. Reprint 2026.

ISBN 978-1-971750-07-1 (paperback)

"O Pen of the Most High!
Say: O people of the world! We have enjoined upon
you fasting during a brief period, and at its close have
designated for you Naw-Rúz as a feast. Thus hath the Day-Star
of Utterance shone forth above the horizon of the Book as decreed
by Him Who is the Lord of the beginning and the end. Let the days
in excess of the months be placed before the month of fasting. We have
ordained that these, amid all nights and days, shall be the manifestations
of the letter Há, and thus they have not been bounded by the limits of the
year and its months. It behoveth the people of Bahá, throughout these days,
to provide good cheer for themselves, their kindred and, beyond them, the
poor and needy, and with joy and exultation to hail and glorify their Lord,
to sing His praise and magnify His Name; and when they end—these days
of giving that precede the season of restraint—let them enter upon
the Fast. Thus hath it been ordained by Him Who is the Lord
of all mankind. The traveller, the ailing, those who are with
child or giving suck, are not bound by the Fast;
they have been exempted by God as a token
of His grace. He, verily, is the Almighty,
the Most Generous. "

Bahá'u'lláh, The Kitáb-i-Aqdas

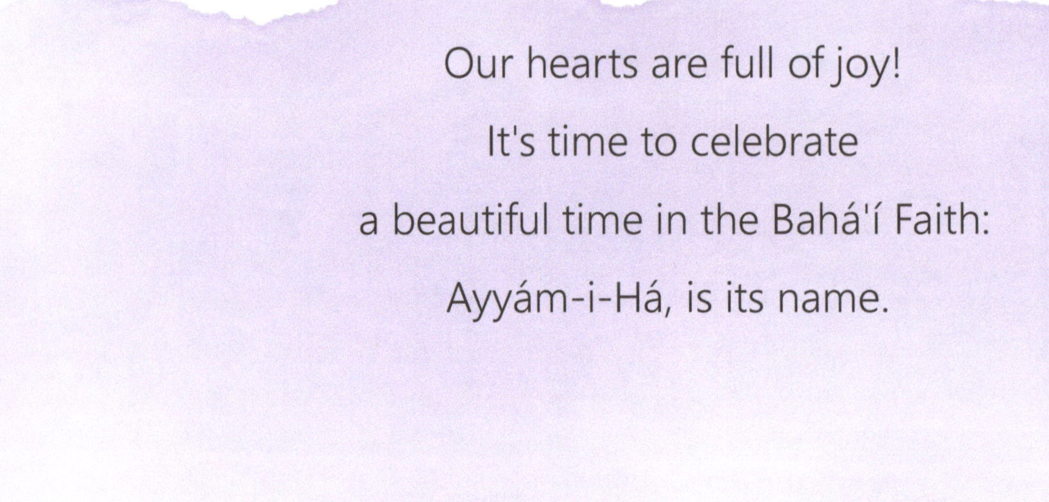

Our hearts are full of joy!

It's time to celebrate

a beautiful time in the Bahá'í Faith:

Ayyám-i-Há, is its name.

Days of Ayyám-i-Há, days celebrated all over the world
by Bahá'í adults, youth, and children like you and me,
with our families, communities, neighbors, and friends.
We send you loving greetings from every corner of the Earth.

या मा हा की खुशी खुशी भधाई हो
(Ayyám-i-Há khushi khushi bhadhai ho)
Hindi, India

Feliz Ayyám-i-Há

As Bahá'ís we believe in unity.

One God, the unity of His Prophets, and the unity of humanity.

Loving one another, serving together,

making the world a better place.

Days of Ayyám-i-Há, days of Há,

days of the Essence of God,

days outside of time, Intercalary Days,

days of joy!

Ayyám-i-há
Pa Anigye Wom

Twi, Ghana

阿亚米哈快乐
(Ayyám-i-Há Kuai Le)
Mandarin, China

Ayyám-i-Há is four to five days long.

In the Badí' calendar of 19 months, each with 19 days,

a few days are left to celebrate

a month before Naw-Rúz, the Bahá'í New Years Day.

Days of Ayyám-i-Há,

days of good cheer, service and exultation,

days that help us prepare for the Fast,

days of joy before restraint, before it's Naw-Rúz again!

ایّام هاء مبارک
(Ayyám-i-Há Mobarak)
Persian, Iran

Felices Días
Intercalares

Spanish,
Puerto Rico

Joyeux Ayyám-i-Há
French, France

С праздником Айам-и-Ха
(S 'prazneekam Ayyám-i-Há)
Russian, Russia

Ayyám-i-Há is a time
for good cheer and rejoicing.
Around the world we enjoy gift-giving
and fellowship with all.

Days of Ayyám-i-Há,
days full of joy and celebration,
days of feasting and hospitality,
days of love to all humanity!

Hery Ayyám-i-Há

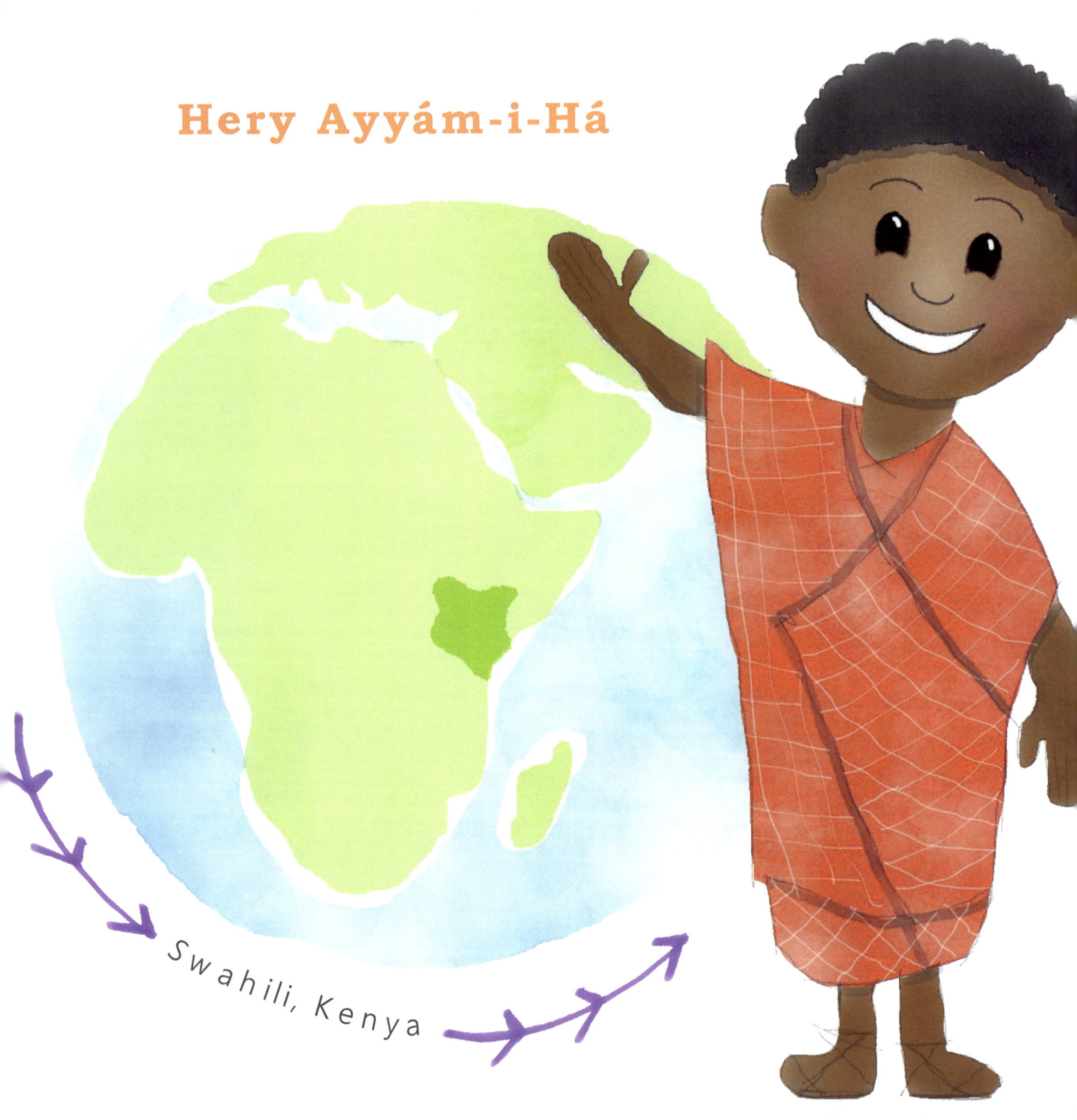

உபரி நாட்கள்
(Ubari Naatkal Valthukkal)
Tamil, Singapore

Ayyám-i-Há is a time
for service and charity.
In every country we assist the poor and needy,
with compassion and love.

Days of Ayyám-i-Há,
days to care for the sick,
days to help the poor,
days to bring cheer to the sorrowful!

Fröhliches
Ayyám-i-Há
German, Germany

Happy
Intercalary Days
English,
United States
of America

Ayyám-i-Há is a time
to glorify God's Name.
Around the world we sing, chant, and recite
beautiful prayers with joy and delight.

Days of Ayyám-i-Há,
days to sing God's praise,
days to magnify and glorify God's Name,
days of good cheer, service, and exultation
are the days of Ayyám-i-Há!

Happy
Ayyám-i-Há

to you!

For further information about the Bahá'í Faith, please visit:

www.bahai.org

References:

Bahá'u'lláh, The Kitáb-i-Aqdas

Bahá'u'lláh; Prayers and Meditations

Various; Bahá'í Prayers: A Selection of Prayers Revealed by Bahá'u'lláh, the Báb, and 'Abdu'l-Bahá

J. E. Esslemont; Bahá'u'lláh and the New Era

Heartfelt Thanks to:
My beloved husband Darioush Charepoo for all his support.

Leanna Guillén Mora for editing the book and helping with proofreading
and illustration proofing.

Sophia Wood for sharing with me your knowledge on
writing, publishing books and helping with proofreading.

Thomas Kavelin, Varya Sanina-Garmroud, Nilmari Donate, Marcela Lemus, and
Rachel Anderson for helping with proofreading.

Elegna Rodríguez and Nilmari Donate for helping with illustration proofing.

To Elika Mahony, Jaleh Ehsani, Kamal Singh, Clement Papafio, Adwoa Ulzen Setrakian,
Varya Sanina-Garmroud, Carmel Irandoust, Katrin Modabber, Amy Brooks, Pamela Douglas,
Kavita Ilangovan and other contributors for helping with the translation of
"Happy Ayyám-i-Há" and "Happy Intercalary Days" in different languages.